TITLE PAGE

A SYSTEMATIC APPROACH TO THE STUDY OF PHOTOSHOP 2022 Teach Yourself Photoshop

Enomfon Emmanuel Nkok

Copyright © 2022
Enomfon Emmanuel Nkok
All rights reserved

The characters and events portrayed in this book are fictitious. Any similarity to real persons, living or dead, is coincidental and not intended by the author.

No part of this book may be reproduced, or stored in a retrieval system, or transmitted in any form or by any means, electronic, mechanical, photocopying, recording, or otherwise, without express written permission of the publisher.
ISBN: 9798352215173

DEDICATION

To Almighty God and to my beloved parents Mr/Mrs. Emmanuel Harry Nkok.

CONTENTS

Acknowledgments

1 Chapter One
2 Chapter Two
3 Chapter Three
4 Chapter Four
5 Chapter Five
6 Chapter Six
7 Chapter Seven

ACKNOWLEDGMENTS

I give almighty God the utmost thanks and honor for giving methe strength, wisdom, and intellectual drive to write this book. Though the journey was not easy but he saw me through.

I am extremely grateful to my friend Happiness Etim whose intellectualcontributions and supports make this book a reality. Without her contribution, this book would have remained a wishful thinking.

My deep appreciation also goes to my parents for sending me to school,which enabled me to get the knowledge and write this book. Without their support and love I would have remained in the village.This dream would never have come to pass.

To my siblings and parents, who bore the deprivation of non-communication doing the period of writing this book. I say a big thank you.

As I sign off, I give the utmost Thanks to God Almighty for hisUnquantifiable Support, love and blessings. As always, to Him be all the Glory.

CHAPTER ONE

Introduction Adobe Photoshop was originally developed in 1987 by the brothers John and Thomas Knoll. Since its original development, Photoshop has evolved from a simple image editing tool to a comprehensive suite for image manipulation. While early versions of Photoshop were produced and distributed by the Knoll brothers, the software was acquired by Adobe Systems and became Adobe Photoshop. The earliest version of the software released by Adobe came in February 1990. It allowed users to display and save files in multiple formats on early MacOS computers. Users could also adjust the hue, balance, and color saturation of images. There were minimal painting capabilities, as well as soft edge selections. Graphic designers were quick to adopt Adobe Photoshop. From the addition of CMYKcolor support and Duotones in Version 2.0 to the new painting engine and vector text of Version 7.0, each version rapidly become more comprehensive than the last.

1.1. Basic Functions of Photoshop

1. You can adjust the saturation of your images The saturation factor of your colors may be adjusted. You can lower the saturation if you think the image is too imposing, or if it is looking a little pale then you can increase the saturation for a fuller look. Increasing the saturation of your image colors for pictures you are going to put on eBay makes the product look more colorful in the thumbnail images.

2. You can adjust the color levels There is often a slider function that allows you to play with the brightness and contrast at the same time. You can play with the levels to see if your image looks better. You can make the picture look a lot brighter and fuller than it actually is in a way that you may not be able to achieve (at least not as well) if you were to adjust the brightness and contrast separately.

3. You can alter the highlights and shadows Most modern photoshop programs allow you to control how bright the highlights and the shadows are. The highlights are the bits where the light hits the objects directly and you may tone them down a little if things look a little too glary. You may also increase the lightness of your shadows so they do not look as looming.

7. You can set the orientation and straightness of the image You can set it to landscape or portrait, and you may also adjust the angle at which the image is set by spinning it on a central axis. This often leaves white

spaces around the edges, so you will need to crop your image once you are done.

8. You can clone areas to remove blemishes The clone tool will take image pixels from a small area near the blemish so that you may paint over it and the blemish disappears. It is easy to become quite proficient at this if you practice a little and keep zooming in and out to see how it looks.

9. You can remove red eye This is very simple and many photoshopping programs will do it automatically for you. The only problem is that red eye has no reflections in it, and any reflection is usually completely gone after the red eye function has worked which leaves you with black and vacant eyes. If this happens you may like to try adding a little texture back into the pupil and maybe even try adding a reflection in there.

10. You can auto-adjust the image
This should really be done for inspiration as to a few changes you should make to the image. There are rare times when the image will look great after an auto-adjust, but the program usually gets an element or two wrong. If it does look okay then consider changing the image after the auto-adjust has done its thing.

1.2. What is Photoshop?
Adobe Photoshop is a software application for image editing and photo retouching for use on Windows or MacOS computers. Photoshop offers users the ability to create, enhance, or otherwise edit images, artwork, and illustrations. Changing backgrounds, simulating a real-life painting, or creating an alternative view of the universe are all possible with Adobe Photoshop. It is the most widely used software tool for photo editing, image manipulation, and retouching for numerous image and video file formats. The tools within Photoshop make it possible to edit both individual images as well as large batches of photos. There are several versions of Photoshop, including Photoshop CC, Photoshop Elements, Photoshop Lightroom and Photoshop Express, a version of Photoshop for iOS with reduced features. Adobe Photoshop is available on its own as a subscription that includes Photoshop Lightroom, and as part of the larger Creative Cloud subscription.

1.3. How is Photoshop Used?
Adobe Photoshop is a critical tool for designers, web developers, graphic artists, photographers, and creative professionals. It is widely used for image editing, retouching, creating image compositions, website mockups, and adding affects. Digital or scanned images can be edited for use online or in-print. Website layouts can be created within Photoshop; their designs can be finalized before developers move on to the coding stage. Stand-alone graphics can be created and exported for use within other programs.

What is Photoshop CC? Adobe Photoshop CC is the Creative Cloud version of Photoshop, available by subscription. It is considered to be the professional-level version of the Photoshop family of products. Photoshop CC is available together with. Photoshop Lightroom, or as part of a larger Creative Cloud subscription. Photoshop CC is an advanced imaging software used by designers, web professionals, video editors, and photographers to alter or manipulate digital images. Photoshop is primarily used to edit 2D images, although it does offer some 3D image editing functionality. Photoshop includes image analysis functionality, and can be used to prepare images for use online or in-print.

What is Photoshop Elements? Adobe Photoshop Elements is the consumer-level version of the Photoshop family of products. Photoshop Elements contains many of the professional capabilities that are found in Adobe Photoshop CC, yet they are provided with more simplistic options

designed with an entry-level user in mind. More specifically, it is designed for amateur photographers and digital photography hobbyists. Photoshop Elements is built using the same core digital imaging technology as Photoshop CC. Commonly used capabilities of Photoshop Elements include:

What is Photoshop Lightroom? Photoshop Lightroom is part of the Photoshop family of products and is primarily used by photographers for batch processing of large volumes of images. Lightroom does have the ability to create and save image presets that can be applied to a large batch of photos at one time. It also features non-destructive imaging tools; so that the original files remain intact. Lightroom has the ability to edit RAW files. The light balance and white exposure can be manipulated or adjusted within a RAW file. However, Photoshop Lightroom does not have many of the operating features or functions of Adobe Photoshop CC or Adobe Photoshop Elements, and uses a different interface.

How much does Photoshop cost? The cost of Adobe Photoshop varies for each specific Photoshop product. Photoshop Elements costs $100 and can be used forever after purchasing it. This software is considered to have a perpetual license. The cost of the other Photoshop products ranges from $10 per month to $60 per month depending upon the type of subscription and the length of the subscription. The lower cost options include the Photoshop-only apps, while the higher cost options include Photoshop along with other Creative Cloud tools. Discounted plans are also available for students, teachers, and organizations looking to purchase licenses for groups of 10 or more employees. How to learn Photoshop There are several ways to learn Adobe Photoshop. Popular methods include taking in-person Photoshop classes, live online Photoshop classes, learning via online Photoshop tutorials, and Photoshop books. Classes are designed to help students benefit from both group learning activities and one-on-one instruction. Classroom learning also has the advantage of helping students overcome challenges or obstacles through guided instruction. These learning opportunities are particularly helpful when new features or tools are released. American Graphics Institute offers Photoshop classes in Boston, as well as New York City and also Philadelphia. Adobe Photoshop training with an online instructor is the ideal solution for students with busy schedules who are not able to travel to a classroom. Online classes offer a hands-on approach to learning that can be particularly beneficial to beginners. They can help first time users navigate all of the features and tools of Adobe Photoshop. From learning how to create paths to understanding which file format should be selected, online instructors can

help beginners quickly become Photoshop experts.

Photoshop Mac vs. Windows Differences
There are very few differences between Photoshop on MacOS vs Windows computers. Menus, options, panels, and tools are found in the same location on both Mac and Windows versions of Photoshop. There is no functionality difference between Adobe Photoshop on a Mac or Windows computers. Before Adobe Photoshop can be used on either Mac or Windows computers, the computer itself must meet the following minimum requirements.

Computer requirements for Photoshop Windows: To use Photoshop on a Windows computer, a computer must meet these requirements: Intel® Core 2 or AMD Athlon® 64 processor; 2 GHz processor or greater. Microsoft Windows 7 with Service Pack 1, Windows 8.1, or Windows 10. 2 GB or more of RAM. 2.6 GB or more of available hard-disk space for 32-bit installation; 3.1 GB or more of available hard-disk space for 64-bit installation; as well as the additional free space required for installation. 1024 x 768 display with 16-bit color and 512 MB or more of dedicated VRAM. OpenGL 2.0-capable system. Internet connection is required to activate software, validate subscriptions, and access various online services. Computer requirements for Photoshop Mac: To use Photoshop on a Mac OS computer, a computer must meet these requirements: Multicore Intel processor with 64-bit support. MacOS version 10.13 (High Sierra), MacOS version 10.12 (Sierra), or Mac OS X version 10.11 (El Capitan). 2 GB or more of RAM. 4 GB or more of available hard-disk space for installation, as well as the additional free space required for installation. 1024 x 768 display with 16-bit color and 512 MB or more of dedicated VRAM. OpenGL 2.0-capable system. Internet connection is required to activate software, validate subscriptions, and access various online services.

Photoshop file formats
Adobe Photoshop can save or export images and graphics in a variety of file formats. These formats are used for different purposes. For example, images used on websites generally need to be small so they can load quickly; while images that are being included in a 3D product rendering may need to be of higher resolution and include additional details. Some images may contain only pixels, while others may contain a mixture of pixels and vectors. A few file formats also use compression techniques to

reduce the size of the image, and certain compression options intentionally discard data to make the file size smaller. In order to preserve all Adobe Photoshop features, including effects, masks, and layers the Photoshop file format (PSD) is used. File formats Photoshop can open or save include: Photoshop Format (PSD) -- PSD files can be up to 2 GB in size. Only Photoshop PSD as the ability to save all elements of the edited image or graphic. Large Document Format (PSB) -- PSB files can be larger than 2 GB in size and support up to 300,000 pixels in any dimension. The applied layers and filters are also supported. Tagged-Image File Format (TIFF) -- This flexible bitmap image format is supported by numerous applications and computer platforms. CMYK, RGB, grayscale, and indexed color are supported. TIFF documents have a maximum file size of 4 GB. If a TIFF file is opened in another application, then only a flattened image will be presented even though the layers have been saved. RAW -- RAW files can be larger than 2 GB in size. RAW files are flexible and can be used to transfer images between computers or applications.

This format does support CMYK, RGB, and grayscale images; however, files must be flattened before saving. Portable Document Format (PDF) -- Fonts, page layouts, vector, and bitmap graphics can be accurately displayed with PDF files. Additionally, electronic links can be included within a PDF file. Up to 16 bits per channel images can be saved without quality degradation. Graphics Interchange Format (GIF) -- This file format is often used to display indexed color graphics or images within a designated HTML document. GIF minimizes file sizes and reduces the electronic transfer time. It does not support alpha channels. Portable Network Graphics (PNG) -- Lossless compression is achieved with PNG. It supports 24 bit images; however, some web browsers do not support PNG files. PNG does preserve transparency in both RGB and grayscale images. It also supports indexed color, grayscale, RGB, and bitmap mode images. Joint Photographic Experts Group (JPEG) -- This file format is often selected for continuous-tone images for HTML documents. It supports grayscale, RGB, and CMYK color modes. It retains all color information within an RGB image, however it compresses the file size by discarding selected data. A JPEG is automatically decompressed when the file is opened. Cineon -- The 10 bits per channel digital format was developed by Kodak. It is used to output back to film without losing image quality. It can be used in the Cineon Digital Film System.

Photoshop CS vs Photoshop CC
The introduction of the Creative Suite branding provided each version of Photoshop with a "CS" followed by a version number after the first version of the Creative Suite. Thus, the versions of Adobe Photoshop after Photoshop CS became Photoshop CS2, then Photoshop CS3, which continued through June 2013. At that time, Adobe introduced a new licensing program in which Photoshop was rented either by the month or year as part of a subscription. At that time, Photoshop CS was replaced by Photoshop CC for Creative Cloud. The Creative Cloud designation is followed by the year in which the application received its most recent update. Photoshop CS: Photoshop CS was released in October 2003. It represented the switch to the Creative Suite branding. Improvements included: the addition of camera RAW 2.0, match color command, real-time histogram palette, increased user control, and the shadow / highlight command.

Photo shop CS2: Released in May 2005, this version featured additional improvements, including: custom presets, an upgraded file browser to Adobe Bridge, non-destructive editing, a lens correction filter, and smart objects. Photoshop CS3: Released in April 2007, this update improved image stitching, offered additional print options, enhanced mobile optimization, and increased the support offered for Camera Raw. Photoshop CS4: Released in October 2008, this version of Photoshop included the following improvements: content-aware scaling, enhanced file management and workspaces, adjustments panel, increases to the Lightroom workflow, and a simplified tab-based interface. Photoshop CS5: Released in April 2010, the following improvements were gained: 64 bit support, color pickup, bristle tips, auto image straightening, a new mixer brush, and the refine edge tool. Photoshop CS6: Released in May 2012, this update provided a redesigned user interface, an auto save feature, revised vector tools, and enhanced video tools, such as the ability to include layers, manipulate color, and adjust exposure levels.

1.4. How to draw shapes with the Custom Shape Tool
There are two ways to draw custom shapes in Photoshop. The first is with the Custom Shape Tool and the second is from the Shapes panel. We'll start by learning the more traditional way of drawing shapes using the Custom Shape Tool.
 Step 1: Select the Custom Shape Tool The Custom Shape Tool is found in Photoshop's toolbar, nested in with the Rectangle Tool, Ellipse Tool and Photoshop's other geometric shape tools. To select the Custom Shape Tool, click and hold on whichever shape tool's icon is currently visible in the toolbar (either the Rectangle Tool or the tool you used last). Then choose the Custom Shape Tool from the fly-out menu. Selecting the Custom Shape Tool from Photoshop's toolbar Selecting the Custom Shape Tool.

Step 2: Open the Custom Shape Picker with the Custom Shape Tool active, go up to the Options Bar and choose a shape by clicking on the current shape's thumbnail. Clicking on the current custom shape in Photoshop's Options Bar Clicking on the current shape in the Options Bar. This opens the Custom Shape Picker showing all the shapes we can choose from. The shapes are divided into groups based on their theme. But by default, only four groups are listed (Wild Animals, Leaf Trees, Boats and Flowers). I'll show you how to load hundreds of additional shapes once we've learned how the Custom Shape Tool works.

Step 3: Choose a custom shape Twirl open a shape group by clicking the arrow to the left of its folder icon. I'll open the Wild Animals group. Then choose a shape from the group by clicking its thumbnail. I'll choose the lion shape.

Step 4: Set the Tool Mode to Shape. Still in the Options Bar, make sure the Tool Mode is set to Shape, not Path or Pixels. Setting the Tool Mode for the Custom Shape Tool to Shape in Photoshop's Options Bar Setting the mode for the Custom Shape Tool to Shape.

Step 5: Choose a fill color Then choose a color for the shape. The default color is black. To choose a different color, click the Fill color swatch. Clicking the Fill color swatch to choose a shape color Clicking the Fill color swatch in the Options Bar. Choose the kind of fill you need using the icons along the top of the panel. From left to right, we have No Color, a Solid Color preset, a Gradient preset, or a Pattern preset. If you choose one of the three preset options, then select a preset from one of the groups below. The No Color, Solid Color preset, Gradient preset and Pattern

preset fill options for the shape. The No Color, Solid Color, Gradient and Pattern preset options for the fill. Or to choose a custom color for your shape, click the icon on the far right. Clicking the custom color icon. Clicking the custom color icon for the fill. Then choose a color from the Color Picker. I'll choose a shade of purple by setting the H (Hue) to 295 degrees, the S (Saturation) to 70 percent, and the B (Brightness) also to 70 percent. Click OK to close the Color Picker. Choosing a fill color for the shape from the Color Picker in Photoshop Choosing a fill color from the Color Picker.

Step 6: Choose a stroke color and size By default, Photoshop adds a 1 pixel-wide black stroke around shapes. To choose a different color, or to turn off the stroke, click the Stroke color swatch in the Options Bar. Clicking the Stroke color swatch for the Custom Shape Tool in Photoshop's Options Bar Clicking the Stroke color swatch in the Options Bar. Then along the top of the panel, choose from the same options that we saw with the fill color. From left to right, click the No Color option to turn off the stroke. Or choose either a Solid Color preset, a Gradient preset or Pattern preset. The stroke color options for the Custom Shape Tool in Photoshop. The stroke color options are the same as the fill options. Or click the icon on the far right to open the Color Picker and choose a custom color. But I'll leave the stroke set to black. The custom color icon for the stroke. The custom color icon for the stroke. In the Size box next to the color swatch, enter a width or thickness for the stroke. I'll set mine to 10 px. Press Enter (Win) / Return (Mac) to accept it. Entering a size for the stroke that will appear around the custom shape Entering a size for the stroke.

Step 7: Choose the stroke type and alignment. If you click the Stroke Options box next to the size value: The Stroke Options box for the Custom Shape Tool. The Stroke Options box. You'll find a few more options you can set before drawing the shape. At the top of the panel, set the stroke's type to either a solid, dashed or dotted line. The default is solid which is usually what you want. And in the bottom left of the panel, set the stroke's align ment to either inside the shape's edge, outside the edge or centered on the edge. The default is centered. You can also change the stroke's cap type and corner type from here, but the defaults are usually fine. The stroke options include the line type, alignment, cap type and corner type.The stroke options include the line type, alignment, cap type and corner type.

Step 8: Draw the shape to draw your custom shape, click on the canvas to set a starting point, keep your mouse button held down, and drag away from that point. As you drag, all you will see is the shape's path outline. Clicking and dragging to begin drawing the custom shape in Photoshop. Click and drag to begin drawing the shape. How to draw the shape at the correct aspect ratio by default, Photoshop lets us draw the shape freely with the aspect ratio unlocked, which can make it look warped. So to force the shape into its correct aspect ratio, press and hold the Shift key on your keyboard as you drag. Holding Shift to draw the custom shape at the proper aspect ratio. Hold Shift to draw the shape at the proper aspect ratio. How to reposition the shape as you draw? To reposition the shape on the canvas as you draw it, press and hold the spacebar on your keyboard. With the spacebar down, drag to move the path outline into place. Then release the spacebar to continue drawing the shape. Hold the spacebar to reposition the custom shape as you draw it. Hold the spacebar to reposition the shape. How to complete the shape. Release your mouse button to finish drawing the shape, at which point the fill color and stroke appear. Release your mouse button to add the fill and stroke to the shape. Release your mouse button to add the fill and stroke to the shape.

Step 9: Resize or rotate the shape Photoshop automatically places a transform box around the shape so we can resize or rotate it if needed. How to resize the shape.To resize the shape, click and drag any of the transform handles (the little squares). Hold the Shift key as you drag a handle to maintain the shape's correct aspect ratio as you resize it. To resize the shape outward from its center rather than from the opposite side or corner, hold the Alt (Win) / Option (Mac) key as you drag a handle. Holding Shift plus the Alt (Win) / Option (Mac) key will lock the shape's aspect ratio and resize it from the center. Resizing the custom shape with the transform handles in Photoshop. Use the transform handles to resize the shape. Hold Shift to lock the aspect ratio.How to rotate the shape To rotate the shape, hover your mouse cursor just outside one of the transform handles. When the cursor changes to a rotate icon (a curved double-sided arrow), click and drag to rotate the shape around its center. Hold Shift as you drag to rotate the shape in 15 degree increments. Dragging outside a transform handle to rotate the custom shape. Drag outside a transform handle to rotate the shape.I'll rotate my shape back to its original angle. Resetting the angle of the custom shape. Resetting the angle..

Step 10: Accept the shape and close the Transform Command Press Enter (Win) / Return (Mac) on your keyboard when you're done to accept it and close the transform box. In the Layers panel, the new shape appears on its own shape layer. And since I chose the lion shape, Photoshop named the layer Lion 1. Photoshop's Layers panel showing the new shape layer. The Layers panel showing the new shape layer. How to edit the shape's fill and stroke Even though we've already drawn the shape, we can always go back and edit the fill color and stroke options as long as the shape layer is selected in the Layers panel. And there's a few places to do it. From the Options Bar. You can go back to the Options Bar and change the fill or stroke using the options we looked at before drawing the shape. Editing the custom shape's fill and stroke in Photoshop's Options Bar Editing the fill and stroke in the Options Bar. From the Properties Panel or you can change the fill or stroke from Photoshop's Properties panel. The fill, stroke and other shape options in Photoshop's Properties panel. The fill, stroke and other shape options in the Properties panel. For example, I don't like the stroke around my shape. So to remove it, I'll click the Stroke color swatch in the Properties panel. Editing the stroke color in the Properties panel. Editing the stroke color in the Properties panel. Then I'll choose the No Color option at the top, just like we saw earlier in the Options Bar.

CHAPTER TWO

2.1. How to start a new document in Photoshop. First of all, double click on your Photoshop to open Photoshop workspace for you. Go to file, new, choose width and height of your project or choose paper size then click ok. Photoshop will automatically create a new document for you, where you can use and start up your new project designs. 2.2. How to Remove and Replace Background.

2.2. Removal Steps
Step 1: open your Photoshop (PS) it will take you to your Photoshop work space, go to your folder where you have your pictures then choose any picture of your choice, drag and drag into your Photoshop workspace or you simply go to file in your window then click open, it will also take you to where you have your picture then click on any picture of your choice and click open. It will also take the picture to your Photoshop workspace.

Step2: Pick your polygonal Lasso tool and start click on the edging of the picture carefully when you are done click rotate it above the picture and outside the workspace, come to where you started and cropping and double on it.

Step3: It will make selection, then right click on your mouse, go to feather, feather it with 2 radius as the case maybe, then go to select by your left hand on your window under select go to modify, expand it, with two pixel depending.

Step 4: Come to your layer and double click on it to unlock it. Why do we unlock layer? We unlock layer in other to be able to work on the background of the picture. When you double click on the background it will open a box which demanded you to click OK then click ok it will automatically unlock the background for you then can now press Delete on your keyboard. It will automatically remove the background for you.

2.3. REPLACEMENT
Create a new layer, change your foreground and background colour and to any colour of your choice, it could be red, blue, green etc. Pick your gradient tool come to the edge of the picture and then drag from right to left to fill colour on the layer, then take the picture above the colour. Your background will automatically replace. Finally, right click on the layer to flatten it.

1.3. How to save. There are different important ways of saving works in Photoshop but we will be talking about four of them in this book.

Photoshop Document (PSD) Photoshop Document is the default fill format of document created in Adobe Photoshop. The PSD format allows a photos user to save all the information needed to continue editing the fill later, such as layers, guides, and transparency masks.

Portable Network Graphics (PNG) It was created as an open file to replace Graphics interchange format (GIF) because the patent for GIF was owned by one company and nobody else wanted to pay licensing fees. It also allows for a full range of colour and better compression.

Joint Photographic Experts Group (JPEG OR JPG) It used to save work as an image formatting. JEPG are images that have been compressed to store a lot of information in a small size file.

Raw Image Files. Raw image files contain data from a digital camera. The files are called raw because they haven't been processed and therefore can't be edited or printed yet. Raw file usually contains a vast amount of data that is uncompressed. Because of this, the size of a raw file is extremely large.

2.4. HOW DO A PASSPORT.

Step 1. Bring in your PNG picture to your Photoshop workspace. Put in red background and flatten it. Go to your file, new, choose the width 32 by 42, resolution 70 click OK.

Step2: Bring in the picture from the layer to the passport layout which you created, then press control T and control plus minus (-) and zoom out the passport to see the full size of it. Press Ctrl, shift and ALT and go to the right top corner angle to reduce or increase the size of the passport proportionally. Double click inside and confirm it. 2.5. How to Blur Background Step 1. Import in the picture that you want to blur.

Step 3. Duplicate the picture twice by pressing Ctrl + J Step 3. Name the first mode, the second one blur, and the third background. Hide the Bur and the background layer.

Step 4. Pick quick selection tool and start clicking on the picture you want to blur. Once the selection is done, , go to your window and click on refine to make the edge smooth, click ok.

Step 5. Come and click on your layer mark then the background will remove automatically. Come and unhide the blur layer.

Step 6. To remove the mode from the background, hold on Ctrl key and click on the layer mask of that mode layer, it will make selection. Then go to select, under select go to modify, go to expand it by 5 or 6 as the case may be.

Step 7. Right click on your mouse. Go to fill, choose content aware, it will take a little time to load. After that press Ctrl + D to deselect the selection. Make sure the cursor is on the blur layer that you laid. Go to filter, under filter go to blur gallery, under blur gallery choose field blur play with the blur size to give you your desire blur level.

Flatten and save the work.

2.5. How to do text effect EG, Gold with text

Step 1: Go to file, click new to create your document. Select width 1600, height 800. Press ok the new document will appear. Change the background to black.

Step 2: Select the text tool, make sure the font is Times New Roman to give you a perfect gold. Type word GOLD then go to your text style and choose bold. Type style 72, white colour since the background is black. If the text style is not okay for your demand, you can press Ctrl + T to resize to your demand.

Step 3: To turn the text to the gold that you wanted, go to your **Fx,** choose gradient overlay and the colour box will appear. Double click on the colour box. Go to the left side and double click again; it will open another colour box. Under the new colour box, on the left side of the colour box double click and choose R-246, G -238, B - 173, then press ok. Go to the right side of the colour box and double click. Choose R -193, G – 172, B - 81. Change the style of the gradient from linear to refract.

Step 4: Still go to that Fx, choose Bevel and Emboss, change the technique to chisel hard. Click on gloss contour and click on the three leg contour. Choose angle - 120%, opacity - 75%, size – fill it completely, depth - 170%.

Step 5: Still go to that FX, choose inner glow, change from screen to multiply. Set opacity 50. Change the colour of the glow by clicking the colour box.

Step 6: Go to FX again, choose outer glow, opacity - 40%, choose the colour box of the outer glow RGB 232, 128, 31, size - 50 - 60% as the case may be.

2.5. How to create a two colour sticker with add water mark

Step 1: Go to your file, select new. Must be in inches. Choose width - 6, height - 4 and choose colour CMYK (cyan, magenta, yellow, key – black and white) if you intended to print the design.

Step 2: To get the colour one side faintly, pick your gradient tool and put it in refracted. Come to the top layer and drag down from right to left. It will give you the colour you needed. But before that you might change your background and foreground colour to the different colour that you want.

For example, you want yellow and white background, you will change the background and foreground colour to yellow and white respectively.

Step 3: Pick your type tool and type a word, arrange it to meet your demand.

Step 4: Go to your picture folder and import in your LOGO if the work need Logo.

Step 5: If the Logo is not PNG Logo but it is one colour background, use magic wand and click on the background and press delete. It will delete off the background to enable you use it for the design. But if the LOGO is a complicated i.e. two colour background; use polygonal lasso tool to remove the background.

Step 6: Position the LOGO in the middle of the work then go to your layer. You will see opacity; reduce it to something like 20% or so.

CHAPTER THREE

3.1. How to a simple create Receipt

Go to your tools bar and click on rectangle tool. Click and drag and drag anywhere in the workspace. Go to the left top corner and choose your fill and stroke colour. When you are done with the tool, press Ctrl G to group them in one folder. Then pick your type tool and click anywhere and type words given to you by the client. When you are done typing, press Ctrl + T to size and resize the text to meet your demand. You can as well change the colour of your text to any colour of your choice. The text will now be duplicated many times and group it into one folder.

Note: *Rectangular tool can be used to create anything*

3.2. Step by step on how to Wrap Text around Circle

Step 1: Go to file and click on new and click ok.

Step 2: Pick your ellipse and hold your shift key and draw in order to get a perfect circle then leave your mouse first before leaving the shift key in order to get a perfect result.

Step 3: Go to your window at the left side of your window and click on the path.

Step 4: Pick your type tool and click on the line of the circle. Allow the arrow to turn to **S** before you type, while typing the text will be wrapping around the circle.

3.3. How to do Text Reflection, Shadow and Spotlight

Go to new and choose width – 1550, height – 870 and resolution – 150 and choose RGB colour and press ok.

Change the background to black. Make sure the foreground is white then press Ctrl + Delete.

Pick the type tool and type the graphics name.

Make the font colour white. Go to text layer and right click and press convert to a smart object.

Go to your fx (Layer style). Choose bevel and emboss then on the lefthand, tick on the contour. Choose style

Style – Column inner bevel

Technique – Chisel hard

Depth – 100

Direction – Up

Size – Your choice

Open your gross contour and choose ring contour and press ok.

Come and create a new layer. Go to view and make sure your ruler and snap are ticked. Come to your left side and drag a ruler and position it in the middle of your workspace.

Go to your elliptical marquee tool. Go to the top of the guide and hold Alt and drag it down to the middle of the text then press Ctrl + delete then come to the layer of elliptical marquee tool and reduce opacity to 20. Press Ctrl and click on text, it will make selection.

Go to select, under select, go to modify, contrast by 6.

Click on layer mark behind the text layer. It will load the contract behind the text layer. Mark all the layers and press Ctrl G in order to group them. Press Ctrl and click on that place that you use to create layer. The new layer that you created. Name it spotlights. Press Ctrl + delete then reduce

the opacity to 40. Go to edit and transform then go to perspective.

Go to the top layer of the transform. Press Alt and drag it inside. Go to filter, under filter, go to blur then under blur go to Gaussian blur and blur it with 100 pixels then press Ctrl H to hide the ruler. Add a layer mark to the spotlight layer. Open your brush tool and make sure the size of the brush is 800 pixels, then press F9 in your keyboard to open your brush preset and make sure that your blur is smooth and press F9 again to close the preset. Brush the spotlight to give a shadow.

Create a new layer and name it shadows and pick the brush tool and reduce the size – 20 pixel, opacity – 90. Hold your shift key and drag it to the right side. Click on the text layer that you group and press and press ctrl J and duplicate it. Name the top one reflection then ctrl T and transform it and right click and flip vertical. Hold your shift key and drag it down a little.

3.4. How to Convert a Picture to Vector Object

Step1: Bring in the picture and unlock the background. Duplicate it and go to your blending options, change it from normal to colour dodge. Press control I to inverse the picture. Go to filter, blur, Gaussian then blur it with 18.3 pixel then press Okay.

Step2: Go to your layer adjustment then the take saturation from right to left. Go back to your picture it will be converted to a vector picture.

3.5. How to do overlapping image.

Step 1: Bring in the picture and the background that you want to overlapping. Pick your rectangular tool and draw it behind the picture, then go and click on your layer styles (FX) it will take you to where you have them, click on stroke it will take you to where stroke dialogue box, choose stroke colour to any colour of your choice and the size as where.

Step2: still on FX go to drop shadow and play with the size, spread, distance and opacity till it meets your demand. Still in on FX choose blending option this time around. When the blending option dialogue appear, you will see two opacities their normal Opacity and fill opacity. Take the fill opacity from right to left all, come to your knockout and change from none to deep then click Okay.

Step3: Come and bring the picture behind the background that imported, make sure the layer is on the picture layer then press control E. it will automatically merge the background and the rectangular shape that you created. Finally, you duplicate the shape and arrange it to meet your need.

3.6. How to do dot outer line

Step1: Import the picture and duplicate it. Pick your quick selection tool and start clicking on the picture from head to down. When you might have done, go to select behind there modify behind there smooth. Smooth it with 2 pixels.

Step2: go to your select again, behind there expand it with 5 radius. Right click inside that selection and click on make work path and choose the number of your choice.

Step3: select pen tool and click on shape on your window. Go to your rectangular tool and click on no colour since it is only the stroke that is needed here. Choose stroke colour and choose dot stroke. The stroke must

be in the outer rather than inside.

CHAPTER FOUR

4.1. How to sharpen image using three Step

Step1: Import the picture duplicate it. Right click on your layer and convert it to a smart object.

Step2: Go to your filter menu, under there sharpen then under there click on unsharpened mask. In the unsharpened mask dialogue box amount is 128, radius 10.0, threshold 6.

Step3: Click on your layer and press control I to inverse the layer. Pick your blush tool and make sure opacity to 100%. Now start blushing on where you want the sharpen not to affect. When done blushing merge them all.

4.2. How to Remove text without Touching Background.

Step1: Import in the background that has the text into your Photoshop. Pick your Magic wand tool or quick selection tool. Hold your shift key if you are using magic wand tool and click on the text, go to select, modify and expand it with 3 radius.

Step2: Go to edit on your top corner of your window, under there go to edit, under there choose content away then the text will be removed automatically. Press control D to deselect the selection. But if the text is too small to use magic wand tool. You can as well use your healing blush to remove the text.

4.3. Introduction to Typography in Photoshop

Typography simply means creating such an impactful and emphatic typeface (text type) that will grab the reader's attention instantly. Many times text generally gets hidden in the background of the website, ad flyers, promotions, and it cannot give as much force to the reader to take the wordings into consideration. So typography, aka the art of creating a lucrative typeface, enables the designer to let the viewer stop and watch important messages. We can be as creative with typeface as we want, out of which this book will explain simple examples of typeface that are suitable for beginners.

Below are the examples to create Typography in Photoshop:
Example 1 – Floral Font Typography
This is a popular effect. Floral effect typography is used in a lot of festive, wedding type designs and flyers. This gives a very subtle yet powerful thematic message and directly gives the viewer a sense of the purpose of that particular font. This effect in itself can be done in a number of ways. I will show how to do it in a quick, easy and colorful manner.

Step 1: Try to download a beautiful picture of roses online. Open a new document by File then New. Now go to File > Place and place our image of roses as shown below.
Step 2: Go to the Horizontal Type tool. Type the text you wish to edit. Hit enter. You can select any font of your choice.

Horizontal Type tool
Step 3: This is an important step. Make sure the roses image layer is on top of the Text layer. Now right-click on the image layer and select Create Clipping Mask option. You will see that the text has obtained the effect of the rose. We can further do a lot of editing using Blending Options but only if it is required.

Example 2
Step 1: Go to File click on New. Since the font is in black background, fill the background layer with black using the Paint Bucket Tool.

Step 2: Select the Horizontal Type tool and type Stranger Things. Now

what's left is to give effects using Blending options.

type text

Step 3: Let the font be in Caps and Bold. Select the Font Style and size as shown in the image.

Caps and Bold

Step 4: While keeping the text layer selected, start making changes in the placement of the text with the help of the Character panel, as shown below. First, change the Tracking value to -100.

Character panel

Step 5: To stretch the text vertically, set the value of the vertical scale to, let's say, 115%. You can set it as per your liking too.

Step 6: Now, the first and the last letter in the actual font is a bit bigger. To set it like that, select the first letter of the word and change its font size to, let's say, 400.

Step 7: Now, we also know that these big letters are aligned together in one line. This can be easily done using the Baseline Shift option right below the Vertical Scale option in the Character Panel. Select the letters and change the Baseline Shift value to, let's say, -50 pt or any that you are comfortable with.

Step 8: Now, I chose to adjust the Kerning or Spacing between the letters for some extra effects. This I did by changing the value of Kerning or character spacing option right below the Font size option. Change the value to 50. Here I would like to note that I had to change the font size again as I was satisfied with a new value while styling my text.

Step 9: After the desired spacing and letter adjustment is achieved, let's start styling the text. Select the Fill value of the Stranger things layer to 0%.

Step 10: Double click on the layer. In the Layer styles option, select Bevel and Emboss. I had to do a lot of hit and trial values to achieve the desired output. These are the effects I altered; kindly set the following values.

Style: Stroke Emboss
Depth: 220
Size: 3
Uncheck the Use Global Lightbox
Angle: 156
Altitude: 37

Gloss Contour: Cone – Inverted
Check the Anti-aliased box
Highlight Mode – Opacity: 35%
Shadow Mode – Opacity: 50%
Typography in Photoshop - 18
Step 11: Hit the Contour option under Bevel and Emboss and set the following values.
Contour: Cove – Deep
Check the Anti-aliased box.
Step 12: Select the Stroke option, and set the following values and change the color value using the color editor as shown below.
Size: 3
Position: Inside
Typography in Photoshop - 20
Step 13: Select the Inner Glow option and set the following values.

Opacity: 50%
Noise: 5%
Color: #ea0f0f
Size: 17
Step 14: Select the Outer Glow option and set the following values.
Opacity: 50%
Noise: 5%
Color: #ea2314
Size: 12
Range: 60%
Step 15: Once we are satisfied with our styling and editing, select the text layer. Right-click the text layer and select Copy Layer Style. This will be helpful in directly styling the small rectangle shapes later.
Step 16: Select the Rounded Rectangle Tool and create 3 rounded rectangle shapes as shown.
Step 17: Now select each layer and right-click on each layer one by one, and select the option Paste Layer style. This will automatically stylize the shapes according to our text layer. Adjust the layers if necessary; we have our stranger things inspired typography ready.

Conclusion

The following examples were chosen to be able to show the designer that typographical effects don't have to be complicated or difficult to create. What is more important to understand is the purpose for which they have to be created and how will typography affect our design. Rest all is just creativity!

4.4. How to match fonts

Import in the image that has the text then pick your rectangular marque tool and draw on the place that has the text. Go to your text on your top corner of your window and click match fonts it will automatically give you the list of font that resemble that one.

4.5. Using the Standard Pen Tool
Step 1. Click and hold the pen icon on the toolbar. A list of available pens will appear.
You can use the standard pen tool to draw any style of line or shape by creating small segments joined by anchor points.
Step 2. Select Pen Tool.
Step 3. Click the first point in your line. We'll start by drawing straight lines. This drops an anchor at that point. Lift your finger after dropping this anchor.
Step 4. Click the next point in the line. This draws a straight line between the two points. This is the first segment of your line or shape.
If you click a point by mistake, you can delete it by clicking it once to select it, then pressing ← Backspace or Del.
Step 5. Click the next point in the line. Another line will appear between the new anchor and the last one you placed.
Continue clicking points until you've finished your line.
Step 6. Close the path. There are a few ways to do this:
If you want to create a complete shape, click the first anchor point to close the path.
If you didn't draw a shape that must be closed, press ⌘ Command (Mac) or Control (PC) as you click anywhere on the canvas that is not on the line.
Step 7. Click and hold the mouse button to create a new (curved) line. The place you click will become the first anchor point, but this time you won't release the mouse button just yet. The steps are slightly different for curved lines, as you'll be setting the slope before actually drawing the line.
Step 8. Drag the mouse in any direction to set the slope. Release the mouse button once you've gone about 1/3rd of the distance of the line you want to draw. You'll see a direction line, which is really just a guide.
Step 9. Create a C or S-shaped curve. Start by holding the mouse over the

place you want this line segment to end, and then choose one of the following:

For a C-shaped curve, click and drag the mouse in a direction that's opposite to the direction line, and then release the mouse button to see the curve.

For an S-shaped curve, click and drag the mouse in the same direction as the first direction line, then release the mouse button.

Step 10. Keep clicking and dragging the mouse between anchors to create more curves.

As with straight lines, if you drop an anchor by mistake, click it once to select it, then press ← Backspace or Del. To adjust a segment, select the Direct Selection tool by clicking and holding the black arrow tool in the toolbar, and then choosing Direct Selection, select the curve to bring up its anchor points, then drag them the desired locations.

Step 11. Close the path when you're finished. You'll close the path the same as you did when you drew a straight line—by clicking the first anchor point, or by holding ⌘ Command (Mac) or Control (PC) as you click a random blank area.

Using the Curvature Pen Tool

Step 12. Click and hold the pen icon on the toolbar. A list of available pens will appear.

The curvature pen tool is a new tool that helps you easily create paths to draw curved lines and shapes. You'll need to be using Photoshop CC 2018 or later to use this tool.

Step 13. Select Curvature Pen Tool. If you don't see this option and are using the latest version of Photoshop, select Essentials as your workspace at the top-right corner of Photoshop.

Step 14. Click the first point in your line. This drops an anchor at that point. Lift your finger after dropping this anchor.

Step 15. Click the next point in the line. This draws a straight line between the two points. The reason the line is straight is because a curve requires at least three anchor points.

Click the next point in the line. As soon as you click, you'll see that the line will curve, using the second anchor to set the angle. Don't worry, you'll be able to reshape the curve.

Continue clicking points until you've finished your line. If you click a point

by mistake, you can delete it by clicking it once to select it, then pressing ← Backspace or Del.

Click and drag an anchor point to reshape the curve. As long as you have the curvature pen tool selected, you can click any of the points you've dropped and drag them in any direction to adjust the angle and shape of the curve.

You can fine-tune the shape even more by placing additional anchor points along the line, and then clicking-and-dragging them to the desired location. Press Esc to when you're finished drawing. This closes the path. You can now create additional curved lines if you wish.

If you want to create a complete shape, click the first anchor point to close the path.

Click and hold the pen icon on the toolbar. A list of available pens will appear.

If you prefer to freehand-draw your lines, this tool is for you. You can click and drag to draw any line or shape as though you were using the paintbrush tool, except you'll be drawing a path with automatically-added anchor points.

The freehand pen has a "magnetic" option that's great for tracing edges.

Select Freeform Pen Tool.

Click and drag to draw with the tool. When you lift your finger from the mouse, the path will automatically close. Now that you've drawn a freeform line, you'll learn how to use the "magnetic" option for this tool. Select Magnetic in the options bar at the top of the screen (optional). This is helpful if you're tracing around an object. This enables the magnetic pen option, which lets you draw a line that "snaps" to the edges of an object. This is useful when tracing or selecting a specific object on another layer. You can adjust the options for the magnetic pen by clicking the small down-arrow to the left of "Magnetic" in the options bar.

Click a point on the object you're tracing. This drops a "fastening" anchor to the edge.

Move the mouse around the object's edges to trace it. Don't hold down the mouse button, just slowly move the cursor as close to the object's edge as possible. As you move the mouse, the line will appear around the object. If the line isn't snapping to the edge of the object properly, you can periodically click around edge as you trace to drop more fastening anchors.

Double-click to close the path. The line you draw now appears around the selected area.

.4.6. How to Do 3d Mockup

Step1: Bring in the already downloaded mockup fill into your Photoshop, come to the layer and double click on your smart layer. It will ask you to press OK then press it.

Step2: Go to file under, click on place it will open your pictures folders to you then choice the design that you want to place on the mock and click place. It will take the design to your Photoshop. When you are done with positioning it. Double click inside the box and press control S. Go to your timeline you will see the design placed on the mockup.

CHAPTER FIVE

5.1. How to Write Text Behind anything

Step 1. Bring in the picture you want to type the text on. Type the text.

Step 2. Go to magic wand tool and hide the text layer, make a selection of the picture by clicking on it. Unhide the text, press the mask and it will load the text behind. Off the change between the text and the mask to be able to move the text freely.

Step 3. To put something behind the text, go to your solid colour and choose colour of your choice. Make it on the white layer then press Ctrl I, it will turn to the normal picture.

Step 4. Picture your smart object tool and draw a line in where you want the colour to appear then press shift + delete, it will appear the colour on the place you draw the line.

5.2. How to Make a Calendar in Photoshop 2022

You can get really creative with the calendar design, but whether you are making an official calendar or a creative one, the method is the same, you just have to do is change the layout.

Making a calendar in Photoshop is basically organizing layers and designing a layout. There will be a lot of copying and pasting, grouping layers, etc. Easy steps but you need to pay close attention to which layer you're working on.

Now find your favorite image and let's get started.

Step 1: Create a new document in Photoshop. It's up to you what size you want the calendar to be, horizontal or vertical.

A commonly used standard size for a calendar is 8.5" x 11", but I'm going to create an A5 size calendar (about 5.8" x 8.2" or 2460 x 1740px).

Step 2: Drag the image you want to use for the calendar into the Photoshop document. If you want to use a solid color background or pattern, simply go to the top menu and select Edit > Fill.

Hit the Command + R shortcut to view the rulers. Click on the ruler and drag to the canvas to make guides.

You can create a rectangle as a reference to be the distance of your artwork to the canvas border.
Repeat the same step for the rest of the borders. For top and bottom borders you can flip the rectangle horizontally.

Step 3: Use the Type Tool to type out the year of the calendar. Let's make a 2022 calendar. See, here I make sure that my content doesn't go past the guides.

Step 4: Create a new group and name it Jan (or January, anything that's easy for you to recognize). This is going to be the monthly calendar template that you'll be duplicating later. For the other months, you simply need to change the month and days.

Step 5: In the Jan group, create a new layer and select the Rectangle tool to create a box for a monthly calendar, then create another narrower rectangle to show the month. For example, this is going to be the January calendar. Now we are going to type in the days of the week. You can use the guide to set the distance from the calendar box to the day of the week initial.

Step 6: Type in the 7 days of the week and use the Align Vertical Centers tool to keep the letters in the same line. Then select distribute horizontal centers to make sure they have the same spacing in between letters. Use the same method to add the days of the month. January 1st, 2022 will be on Saturday, so I put 1 under Saturday. You can delete the rectangle now. January has 31 days, so you can duplicate the number 30 times, move them to the right positions and then change the numbers. Once you're done, select all days of the month and group them. You can name it days.

Step 7: Duplicate the January (Jan) group and name it Feb. The January template should be in the group folder. Select the February folder and move to the right. Change the month to February and the days. Repeat the same steps. Duplicate the folder, change the name and dates until you finish all the months of the year. That's about it. If you want to show more background image. You can lower the opacity of the calendar box (rectangle) layers.

Conclusion

The most important step of making a calendar is to create the first template, in this case, the month of January. Later on, you only need to move the dates around and change the name of the month.

5.3. How to improve photo image quality from low to high quality

Step 1. Import the image and duplicate it, then go to image, under go to image size.

Width 3000

Height

Resolution 300

Change to pixel.

Step 2. Go to filter under it, go to noise under it go to reduce noise, click on it, it will load and **open.**

Strength 9

Preserve details 16

Reduce color noise 100

Sharpen detail 25.

5.4. How to do a Complete Removal of Noise and Grains

Step 1. Import the picture and duplicate it.

Step 2. Go to filter, from there go to noise under it, reduce noise.

You will see strength 100%

Preserve 0

Reduce colour noise 90

Sharpen details 0%

Then click Okay.

Step 3. Duplicate that one. Go to filter again, under there go to blur, under blur, go to surface blur.

Radius 5%

Threshold 15%

Step 4. Go to filter, under it, go to sharpen, under render, go to smart sharpen.

Amount 90% or more

Radius 1%

Remove: change from lens blur to Gaussian blur.

Step 5. Group the two layer and reduce opacity to 170, and leave the mask for the group layer.

Pick your brush tool and start brushing the eyes of those affected.

5.4. How to improve Picture Quality using High pass

Step 1. Go to edit, under there, preference and Technology preview. Enable the preview details.

Step 2. Go to image. image size, Resolution 300 and width 3000.

Step 3. Go to filter, sharpen and unsharp mark.

Step 4. Press control plus to duplicate. Go to filter, blur and surface blur, adjust a little.

Step 5. Duplicate again. Go to filter, other and highpass, change the blending mode to overlay.

Press Ait and click on the mask.

Make sure the foreground is white, then apply the effect in the area you like to. Done.

5.5. How to Reflective Text

Step 1. Write the text, open your gradient tool.

Open the gradient preset. Click the black and white.

Step 2. Go to the right side of the text, press hold + shift, and click on the text, it will add a new layer behind the text layer.

Step 3. Group the text and duplicate it.

Step 4. Name the second one reflection.

Step 5. Transform the text, go to flip vertical.

Step 6. Drag the text down.

Step 7. Reduce opacity to 25%

Step 8. Click layer mask and make layer next to it.

Step 9. Go to the button of the text and press G to open back your gradient.

Step 10. Press hold+ shift to where you want the reflection to take place.

Step 11. Press control + A to center your wor

CHAPTER SIX

6.1. How to Make a Logo in Photoshop
Does creating a logo yourself seem like a difficult task? Well, it doesn't have to be!
There's plenty of digital art software available like Photoshop, which lets you create a logo —even if you have no logo design experience. In this book, we're going to show you how to use Photoshop to design your very own logo, regardless of your skill level or proficiency with the software. By the end of your reading, you'll have learned how to make a logo using shape tools, color gradients, and font design. Before designing anything, however, it's important to brainstorm some ideas. Jot down notes and even some sketches of what you have in mind, so you have something to base your work on. It will serve as a point of reference that you can peek at during the logo design process and make sure your work aligns with your vision.

1. Create a new canvas.
The very first step on your logo design journey is to create a blank canvas. We recommend that you change the measurement to Pixels, and use a canvas size of at least 500px by 500px. Pixels (px) is a measurement that is universally known in the design world.
You can use a large or smaller canvas size if you want, but this is a decent size to start working with. If you want to change your canvas size, you can do so at any time by going to the canvas properties and manually changing the Height and Width.

2. Create a save file.
Always, always, always (we said it 3 times, so it must be important) create a save file. You never know when the unthinkable will happen, such as spilling a cup of coffee all over your laptop (been there!), and you want to make sure your work is saved. One of the great things about Photoshop is you can save directly to Adobe cloud. This means that even if your laptop goes up in flames and disintegrates into a thousand tiny pieces, you can still access your logo design from another computer. Click on File, then Save As, and choose to save in the Adobe cloud. If you're feeling brave,

you can save your logo design on your computer's hard drive.
3. Draw a basic shape.
To draw a basic shape, choose the Pen tool from the Toolbar. You can also press the shortcut P. Make sure it's set to Shape in the options bar, and not Path.

Note: We also recommend you turn on the grid, as it makes the drawing process much more manageable. Look to the upper-right hand corner, and you'll see a magnifying glass that lets you search instead of hunting through all the different options. Type in Grid, and when it shows up in the search bar, you'll see the shortcut available, and simply click on it to turn it on. Now that the grid is on, let's draw an arrow shape with the pen. Start by clicking on the top point of the canvas, then click on 3 more points to create the design. You can create whatever shape you want here, but to help you get comfortable with Photoshop, you can follow along with our design.

4. Improve the design by duplicating it.
At the moment, our logo doesn't look like much, but this is just the beginning. Using our basic arrow, we're going to duplicate it to create an intricate snowflake design with a cool color gradient.

Design suites like Photoshop use layers to make your job easier. It allows you to place different elements on top of each other to create beautiful effects. The arrow we produced is one layer, and we can freely edit and manipulate it.

Head over to the right-hand side, and inside of the Layers panel, right-click on the arrowhead layer and select duplicate.

If you make a mistake or want to undo something, press CTRL + Z.

5. Add a color gradient.
Color plays an important role in logo design. To make our logo pop, we're going to use a color gradient.

Now, gradient logos are somewhat controversial, in that they remind some designers of the cringey WordArt phase of design. However, if it works for Instagram and Airbnb, it can work for us!

To create a new gradient in Photoshop, click on Fill in the top menu, select New Gradient, and choose from any of the premade ones or create your own.

Now, to get the effect we want, choose a gradient, and for the second layer, reverse it with the reversal button in the bottom-right corner of the fill window.

6. Create a group, and duplicate multiple layers.
Our logo is starting to take shape, but we've still got some work to do.

Group our 2 layers together by selecting them both, and pressing the group button, or CTRL + G. Grouping makes it easier to handle multiple layers at once. Duplicate the new group, and with the Free Transformation tool, CTRL + T, we're going to turn it 180 degrees. Holding down the shift key will cause the rotate symbol to appear; now drag the group to turn it. Once it's turned upside down, we're going to let go. Do this 2 more times, until you have 4 elements pointing towards each other.

7. Create space, and duplicate again.
You can create space in the middle of your shape by moving each shape slightly away from the center. Then, create a new group that consists of all 4 layers and duplicate it. Turn the duplicate shape 45 degrees, and we've got a snowflake! You can duplicate your groups as many times as you like.

8. Add a circle with the shape tool.
Using the Shape Tools, we're going to add a circle. Head over to the Shape Tools icon, right-click, and select the circle. Navigate to the center of your logo design, and hold down ALT to start drawing a circle.

Then, you can change the color of the circle to white if you want to create a nice big space in the middle of your logo.

9. Add a rectangle and center it.
Using the Shape Tool again, choose a rectangle this time and create a white box.

This is where our logo text is going to go. To align it in the center automatically, use the Align tools from the menu bar or the Align Buttons in the options bar.

9. Add text.
To add text to your logo, click on the T icon, which is the Text Box tool in the toolbar, or press T.

Then, drag a text box across the screen to create it. Type your desired text (i.e. your brand name).

10. Choose your font and colors.

It's essential to choose a typeface that represents your brand. Serif, sans-serif, or curved fonts can drastically change your logo's look and feel, so experiment freely until you find the perfect font.

Make sure that you legally own your font, and that you can use it for commercial use in order to avoid trouble down the line.

11. Make adjustments.

You have plenty of room to make any edits or adjustments as needed, such as changing the color, shape, or even duplicating again and adding more elements. When you're happy with your final design, save it in the format you require, and feel free to come back and edit it at any time

CHAPTER SEVEN

Insert chapter seven text here. Insert chapter seven text here. Insert chapter seven text here. Insert chapter seven text here. Insert chapter seven text here. Insert chapter seven text here. Insert chapter seven text here. Insert chapter seven text here. Insert chapter seven text here. Insert chapter seven text here. Insert chapter seven text here.

Insert chapter seven text here. Insert chapter seven text here. Insert chapter seven text here. Insert chapter seven text here. Insert chapter seven text here. Insert chapter seven text here. Insert chapter seven text here. Insert chapter seven text here. Insert chapter seven text here. Insert chapter seven text here. Insert chapter seven text here. Insert chapter seven text here.

Insert chapter seven text here. Insert chapter seven text here.

Insert chapter seven text here. Insert chapter seven text

here. Insert chapter seven text here. Insert chapter seven text here. Insert chapter seven text here. Insert chapter seven text here. Insert chapter

Photoshop shortcuts

Have you ever wasted an entire day in Photoshop? So have I. It's not like you start out aimlessly. You have a simple goal in mind, like cropping a photo, improving the resolution, or changing the size of the canvas. But then, you see all the options. And before you know it, you're attempting to solve The Riddle of the Sphinx.

Wouldn't it be nice if you could just press a button, and magically, Photoshop would do what you wanted it to do? It turns out there are a wealth of Photoshop shortcuts that do exactly this.

By pressing a few keys on your computer keyboard at the same time, you can select tools, manipulate images and layers, and even make adjustments to your project's canvas. This book will teach you how to do all of that (and more) in this guide.

71 Photoshop Shortcuts to Save You Time
Change image size
Change canvas size
Zoom in
Zoom out
Scale Proportionately
Scale in place
Show Rulers
Show or hide the grid
Pointer, a.k.a. Move Tool
Magic Wand
Rectangular Marquee, a.k.a. the Select Tool
Lasso

You'd think setting up your content in Photoshop would be second nature. But sometimes, the shortcuts to change the background size, or zoom into your project aren't what you think. Here are some of the most crucial fundamental shortcuts to know:

Photoshop Shortcuts:
1. Change image size
Control + Alt + I (Command + Option + I)

2. Change canvas size Control + Alt + C (Command + Option + C)
3. Zoom in Control +
4. Zoom out Control -
5. Scale Proportionately
Hold the shift key while selecting the object
6. Scale in place (from center of the object)
Hold shift + option while selecting the object
7. Show Rulers Control + R (Command + R)
8. Show or hide the grid (the automatically-generated horizontal and vertical lines that help align objects to the canvas.) Control + ' (Command + ')

Choosing the Right Tools
These shortcuts will activate different groups of tools, like "Lasso," "Brush," or "Spot Healing Brush." Within these tools, though, there are different functions. Under the "Magic Wand" tool group, for example, you have the option to execute a new selection or add and subtract from a current one.
Each one of these tools has a keyboard shortcut, and we've outlined some of them below.

Photoshop Shortcuts: Choosing the Right Tools
9. Pointer, a.k.a. Move Toolpointer-tool.png **V**
10. Magic Wandmagic-wand-tool.png **W**
11. Rectangular Marquee, a.k.a. the Select Toolmarquee-tool-1.png **M**
12. Lassolasso-tool.png **L**
13. Eye dropper eyedropper-tool. PNG I
14. Crop Screen Shot **C**
15. Eraser **E**
16. Rectanglerectangle-tool.png **U**
17. Horizontal Typetext-tool.**PNG T**
18. Brush **B**
19. History Brush **Y**
20. Spot Healing Brush J
21. Gradient **G**
22. Path Selection **A**
23. Hand **H**
24. Rotate View **R**

25. Pen **P**
26. Clone Stamp **S**
27. Dodge **O**
28. Zoom Tool **Z**
29. Default Foreground and Background colours **D**
30. Switch Foreground and Background Colours **X**
31. Edit in Quick Mask Mode **Q**
32. Change Screen Mode **X**
33. Full Screen **F**

Using the Brush Tool
With the brush settings, you can change the size, shape, and transparency of your brush strokes to achieve a number of different visual effects. To use these keyboard shortcuts, first select the Brush tool by pressing B. Brush
34. Select previous or next brush style , or .
35. Select the first or last brush style used **Shift + , or .**
36. Display precise crosshair for brushes
Caps Lock or Shift + Caps Lock (Caps Lock)
37. Toggle airbrush option **Shift + Alt + P (Shift + Option + p)**

Using the Marquee Tool (for Slicing/Selecting)
When used correctly, the marquee tool will let you select individual elements, entire graphics, and determine what is copied, cut, and pasted into your graphics. To use these keyboard shortcuts, first select the Marquee tool by pressing **M**.
Photoshop Shortcuts: Using the Marquee Tool
38. Toggle between Slice tool and Slice Selection tool
Control (Command)
39. Draw square slice **Shift + drag**
40. Draw from center outward **Alt + drag (Option + drag)**
41. Draw square slice from center outward **Shift + alt + drag (Shift + option + drag)**

42. Reposition the slice while creating the slice **Spacebar + drag**

Using Different Blending Options
Blending options include a number of features to enhance the look of your graphic. You can always choose a blending option by going to the top menu bar, under Layer > Layer Style > Blending Options. Or, you can double-click any layer to bring up the options for that particular layer.
Once you open blending options, you can use keyboard shortcuts to select them without moving your mouse. To use the shortcuts, select the Move tool ("v"), and then select the layer you'd like to use the blending options on. Below are some of the most popular modes.

43. Cycle through blending modes
Shift + + or −
44. Normal mode Shift + **Alt + N (Shift + Option + N)**
45. Dissolve
Shift + Alt + i (Shift + Option + I)
46. Darken
Shift + Alt + k (Shift + Option + K)
47. Lighten
Shift + Alt + g (Shift + Option + G)
48. Multiply
Shift + Alt + m (Shift + Option + M)
49. Overlay
Shift + Alt + o (Shift + Option + O)
50. Hue
Shift + Alt + u (Shift + Option + U)
51. Saturation
Shift + Alt + t (Shift + Option + T)
52. Luminosity
Shift + Alt + y (Shift + Option + Y)
Manipulating Layers & Objects

If you want to modify an object or get complex with multiple layers, here are some shortcuts you might like to know:
53. Select all objects.
Control + a (Command + D)
54. Deselect all objects.

Control + d (Command + D)
55. Select the inverse of the selected objects.
Shift + Control + I (Shift + Command + I)
56. Select all layers.
Control + Alt + a (Command + Option + A)
57. Merge all layers.
Control + Shift + E (Command + Shift + E)
58. **Select top layer. Alt + . (Option + .)**
59. **Select bottom layer. Alt + , (Option + ,)**

Note: In shortcuts 55-57, the brackets ([ ]) are the keystrokes in the command, and "OR" refers to the actual word — as in, press one bracket OR the other, not the letters "O" and "R."
60. Select next layer down or up
Alt + [OR] (Option + [OR])
61. Move target layer down or up
Control + [OR] (Command + [OR])
62. Move layer to the bottom or top
Control + Shift + [OR] (Command + Shift + [OR])
63. Create a new layer
Shift + Control + N (Shift + Command + N)
64. Group selected layers
Control + G (Command + G)
65. Ungroup selected layers
Control + Shift + g (Command + Shift + G)

66. Merge and flatten selected layers
Control + e (Command + E)
67. Combine all layers into a new layer on top of the other layers
Control + Shift + Alt + E (Command + Shift + Option + E)

Note: This step gets you one, combined layer, with all elements of that layer in separate layers below — which is different from a traditional merge-and-flatten layers command.
68. Transform your object (includes resizing and rotating)
Control + t (Command + T)
69. Multiple Undos

Control + Alt + Z (Command + Option + Z)
And Finally — Save Your Work for Later
You've finished working on your project, and now, you're ready to share it with the world. Save time-saving your project by using these simple shortcuts:
Photoshop Shortcuts: Save For Later
70. Save as
Control + Shift + s (Command + Shift + S)
71. Save for web and devices
Control + Shift + Alt + S (Command + Shift + Option + S)

REFERENCES:

Most used shortcuts in Photoshop
https://www.google.com/url?q=https://blog.hubspot.com/marketing/photoshop-keyboard-shortcuts-list&sa=U&ved=2ahUKEwjhtvWLo4P6AhVdgf0HHYlqC_8QFXoECAAQAg&usg=AOvVaw0YwTIhlituY_bgKpJmMR-R

How to create custom shapes
https://www.photoshopessentials.com/basics/how-to-draw-custom-shapes-in-photoshop/

How to use pen tool
https://www.wikihow.com/Use-the-Pen-Tool-in-Photoshop

Typography
https://www.educba.com/typography-in-photoshop/

Creating calendar
https://www.photoshopbuzz.com/how-to-make-calendar/

Creating logo
https://www.google.com/url?q=https://www.tailorbrands.com/blog/how-to-make-a-logo-in-photoshop&sa=U&ved=2ahUKEwiMi8a9rYP6AhV6h_0HHfzZDb4QFnoECAYQAg&usg=AOvVaw3nYXOpW-tD2tst__uLTHtj

What is Photoshop
https://www.agitraining.com/adobe/photoshop/classes/what-is-photosho

www.ingramcontent.com/pod-product-compliance
Lightning Source LLC
Chambersburg PA
CBHW050311220526
45465CB00005B/1936